# Parenting Boys With ADHD

The Complete Guide to Manage Behavioral Problems, Improve School Performance, Teach Social Skills and Prepare Your Child for Success

Linda Hill & Sarah Davis

© Copyright 2023 - All rights reserved.

The content contained within this book may not be reproduced, duplicated or transmitted without direct written permission from the author or the publisher.

Under no circumstances will any blame or legal responsibility be held against the publisher, or author, for any damages, reparation, or monetary loss due to the information contained within this book, either directly or indirectly.

**Legal Notice:**

This book is copyright protected. It is only for personal use. You cannot amend, distribute, sell, use, quote or paraphrase any part, or the content within this book, without the consent of the author or publisher.

**Disclaimer Notice:**

Please note the information contained within this document is for educational and entertainment purposes only. All effort has been executed to present accurate, up to date, reliable, complete information. No warranties of any kind are declared or implied. Readers acknowledge that the author is not engaged in the rendering of legal, financial, medical or professional advice. The content within this book has been derived from various sources. Please consult a licensed professional before attempting any techniques outlined in this book.

By reading this document, the reader agrees that under no circumstances is the author responsible for any losses, direct or indirect, that are incurred as a result of the use of the information contained within this document, including, but not limited to, errors, omissions, or inaccuracies.

# Table Of Content

Introduction ................................................................. 1

**Chapter 1: Understanding ADHD in Boys** ............. 4

But what exactly is ADHD? ........................................... 4

Types of ADHD ............................................................. 5

Unraveling ADHD Symptoms ........................................ 8

The importance of early diagnosis and intervention ..... 12

**Chapter 2: Managing Behavior in Boys with ADHD** ..... 16

Effective discipline strategies for Boys with ADHD ..... 16

Techniques for managing impulsive and hyperactive behavior ... 26

The Role of Medication in Managing ADHD Symptoms ........... 29

**Chapter 3: Improving School Performance in Boys with ADHD** .......................................................... 32

Common academic challenges ....................................... 33

Strategies for improving attention and focus in the classroom ... 39

8 Tips for organizing and completing homework assignments ... 47

## Chapter 4: Teaching Social Skills to Boys with ADHD ..51

Common social challenges for boys with ADHD ........................ 52

6 Techniques for teaching communication and social interaction skills .................................................................................................. 61

Strategies for building self-esteem and positive relationships ...... 73

## Chapter 5: Preparing Your Child for Success in School and Life ................................................................................80

5 Tips for developing resilience and coping skills ........................ 81

Fostering independence and self-advocacy ................................ 91

Additional Resources ...................................................................... 95

## Conclusion ................................................................ 104

## Thank You ................................................................ 107

# Introduction

This is a book dedicated to all the parents, guardians, teachers, and caregivers who strive to understand, support, and empower their exceptional boys every day.

Picture this: your mornings resemble a scene from an action comedy, with socks flying through the air and breakfasts forgotten amidst the morning frenzy. Homework time can easily turn into an epic battle against distraction, where a ten-minute task stretches into hours of wrangling focus. And those moments of sitting still? Well, they seem to belong to l another dimension entirely.

Sound relatable?

In this book, we will embark on an adventure together, exploring the dynamic world of parenting boys with attention-deficit/hyperactivity disorder (ADHD). Drawing from the latest research, expert opinions, and the collective wisdom of parents who have been in the trenches, I will equip you with practical strategies, heartwarming anecdotes, and the tools you need to navigate this adventure with confidence and compassion.

I mean, raising a boy or boys with ADHD is pretty daunting. It is like having a perpetual tornado of energy swirling around your house, leaving chaos in its wake. Keeping their attention focused feels like trying to get a swarm of bees back into their hive. And just when you think you have a moment of peace, their impulsive nature takes them on a spontaneous energy burst, doing anything and everything to keep you on your toes. It is a constant frenzy of managing their never-ending energy, helping them navigate impulsivity, and finding unique and fun ways to keep them engaged. But through all these challenges, you know that if you can just scratch the surface, there is so much potential to be unleashed.

This is not a book about fixing or curing your child. Instead, it is about embracing their neurodivergence, nurturing their strengths, and celebrating the amazing people they are meant to become. My goal is to make readers realize that ADHD is not some horrid disorder that stunts a child's development, that it is in fact, a superpower in its own right. This book will show you how ADHD can actually be your son's greatest asset when going through life.

# Introduction

After having read this book, you will be able to understand what ADHD in boys can look like, and how it might be different from other kinds of ADHD diagnosis. You will get to learn tips and tricks to manage and regulate the behavior of your ADHD boy. You will be able to look into the role that medication plays in ADHD management and find an abundance of valuable information on improving both the practical and social skills of your child.

So, if any of this sounds like something you have been through, or something you would like to learn more about, put your zero-judgment caps on and take this journey with me. Together, we will unravel the mysteries surrounding ADHD and learn to use the "flaws" as weapons that will help our kids navigate through life. Gone are the days when being different was frowned upon - we live in an age that celebrates uniqueness and ADHD is nothing more than that - A unique aspect of one's personality.

## Chapter 1

# Understanding ADHD in Boys

Did you know that ADHD is one of the most common neurodevelopmental disorders? According to statistics, it affects around 5-10% of children worldwide. That means in a classroom of 30 students, there is at least one to two boys who will be navigating the challenges of ADHD. While boys tend to be diagnosed with ADHD more frequently than girls, it is important to remember that ADHD can affect individuals of any gender.

## But what exactly is ADHD?

Picture a bustling rainforest of neural connections in the brain. In children with ADHD, some of these connections will be different, like hidden paths, which makes it harder for them to pay attention, control impulses, and manage their energy levels.

This unique brain wiring sets them apart, and should not be seen as a weakness, but as an aspect of their incredible individuality.

# Types of ADHD

ADHD is commonly classified into three subtypes: predominantly inattentive, predominantly hyperactive-impulsive, and combined presentation. It is important to note that these subtypes are not fixed categories, and symptoms can change and evolve over time. Our boys' ADHD journey may involve a combination of these subtypes, and their experiences are as unique as their individual personalities.

While all three subtypes can affect boys, statistics show that the combined presentation is more prevalent in boys than the other subtypes.

1. **Predominantly Inattentive:**

This subtype is often characterized by difficulties with sustaining attention, staying organized, and following through with tasks. Boys with this subtype may appear dreamy, forgetful, and easily distracted. It is like having a brain filled with fascinating thoughts, but the challenge lies in keeping them in focus.

## 2. Predominantly Hyperactive-Impulsive:

This subtype is characterized by hyperactivity and impulsivity. Boys with this subtype may struggle with sitting still, constantly fidgeting, or tapping their feet. They might act before thinking, blurting out answers, and finding it challenging to control their impulses. It is like having an internal motor that's always revving, making it a thrilling, yet sometimes challenging, ride.

## 3. Combined Presentation:

Boys with the combined presentation experience challenges with both inattention and hyperactivity-impulsivity. They may exhibit symptoms of inattention, such as difficulty focusing and staying organized, as well as symptoms of hyperactivity and impulsivity.

Understanding the subtypes of ADHD can provide valuable insights into the specific challenges our boys may face. By recognizing and embracing their unique strengths and struggles, we can navigate the ADHD jungle with greater empathy, support, and understanding. So, let us celebrate the vibrant diversity within the ADHD spectrum and embark on this adventure with our incredible boys!

Let us take a closer look at how ADHD can impact boys specifically

- Academic challenges can be a formidable part of their journey. Statistics show that boys with ADHD may have lower grades and are at a higher risk of academic difficulties. They may need help focusing during class, completing assignments, and following instructions.

- The social realm can also be challenging terrain for our boys. Research indicates that they may experience higher rates of peer rejection and social difficulties compared to their peers. Impulsivity and hyperactivity might create hurdles in forming and maintaining friendships. But worry not, we'll discover ways to help them forge meaningful connections and thrive in their social interactions.

- Emotional well-being is another vital aspect to consider in the ADHD jungle. Boys with ADHD might experience heightened emotional intensity and difficulty managing their emotions. Frustration, anger, and impatience can be common companions. Understanding and supporting them as they navigate their emotions will be essential for their overall well-being.

As we embark on this adventure through the ADHD jungle, let us remember that every child's journey is unique. While statistics and facts help shed light on the broader picture, it is essential to embrace the individuality of each boy with ADHD. With understanding, support, and a touch of adventure, we can navigate the challenges and celebrate the strengths of our boys with ADHD.

## Unraveling ADHD Symptoms

Picture a diverse ecosystem of symptoms that intertwine to form the complex landscape of ADHD. These symptoms can be categorized into three main areas: hyperactivity, impulsivity, and inattention. While each boy's journey is as unique as the patterns in a jungle, understanding these symptoms will help us navigate through their challenges more effectively.

- **Hyperactivity:**

In the ADHD jungle, hyperactivity reigns supreme. Our boys may seem like they have an infinite supply of energy, constantly on the move. They might find it challenging to sit still for extended periods, often feeling the irresistible urge to fidget, squirm, or tap their feet. You might notice them bouncing from one activity to another like monkeys swinging from branch to branch. Hyperactivity in ADHD is not merely being active; it is an intensity of movement that sets them apart.

- **Impulsivity:**

Impulsivity is the curious creature lurking in the shadows of the

ADHD jungle. Our boys sometimes act before they think, driven by their boundless enthusiasm and zest for life. They might have difficulty controlling their impulses, blurting out answers without raising their hands, or interrupting conversations with their unrestrained excitement. It is like a hidden current that can carry them away, making it a challenge to navigate social interactions and adhere to rules. But remember, impulsivity is not a reflection of disrespect—it is an integral part of their unique neurological makeup.

- **Inattention:**

Among the lush foliage of the ADHD jungle, inattention looms as a significant challenge for our boys. Their attention may wander like a lost explorer, making it difficult to stay focused on tasks or conversations. They may struggle with listening attentively, overlooking details, or getting easily distracted by the myriad stimuli around them. As a result, following instructions, organizing their thoughts, or completing assignments might feel like navigating a dense thicket.

Now that we have gone over some of the more common symptoms, let us get into the specifics. I understand that each boy is different and so their experiences will reflect their uniqueness. However, this table includes most symptoms that have been researched over the years.

As you go over the table, feel free to grab a pen and check off the symptoms that you think your son(s) have shown.

| Hyperactivity symptoms | Impulsivity symptoms | Inattention symptoms |
|---|---|---|
| ✓ Constant restlessness and difficulty staying seated.<br>✓ Fidgeting, squirming, or tapping hands or feet.<br>✓ Excessive talking and difficulty engaging in quiet activities.<br>✓ Running or climbing excessively, even in inappropriate situations. | ✓ Acting without thinking, frequently interrupting others.<br>✓ Difficulty waiting for their turn in activities or conversations.<br>✓ Impatience and a tendency to blurt out answers before the question is complete.<br>✓ Engaging in risky or impulsive behaviors without considering potential consequences. | ✓ Difficulty sustaining focus on tasks, easily getting distracted.<br>✓ Frequently making careless mistakes in schoolwork or other activities.<br>✓ Struggling to follow instructions or complete tasks that require mental effort.<br>✓ Forgetfulness, losing items necessary for tasks or activities. |

## Understanding ADHD in Boys

| Organizational and time management difficulties | Poor impulse control and emotional regulation | Academic and executive function challenges |
| --- | --- | --- |
| - Trouble with organizing tasks, belongings, and schoolwork.<br>- Procrastination and difficulty initiating or completing tasks.<br>- Forgetfulness and frequently losing or misplacing things. | - Difficulty managing emotions, and experiencing intense emotional reactions.<br>- Impulsive outbursts of anger or frustration.<br>- Overreacting to situations or having difficulty handling disappointments.<br>- Impaired ability to self-regulate behavior in different social contexts. | - Struggles with sustained attention and focus in the classroom.<br>- Inconsistent academic performance, often underachieving compared to potential<br>- Difficulties with organization, time management, and planning.<br>- Challenges with completing homework or assignments on time. |

# The importance of early diagnosis and intervention

The journey of parenting is full of twists and turns, and when it comes to ADHD, early detection and timely intervention can make a world of difference. So, let us gather our wisdom and embark on this enlightening discussion together.

As parents, we hold the key to unlocking our child's potential, and early intervention plays a crucial role in ensuring their bright future. In the past, the "wait and see" approach was often favored, with the hope that children would outgrow their challenges. While children develop at different paces, we now know that early intervention for ADHD can be life-altering, just like other therapies such as speech or physical therapy. By understanding the practices and strategies specific to parenting and teaching children with ADHD, we can shield them from negative behaviors and habits that may develop later on.

As previously mentioned, children with ADHD often face social and learning difficulties. A proactive approach helps protect their self-esteem and self-image from potential bruises down the road. When parents are educated about how ADHD can impact their children, they can closely monitor their progress and establish a special protective bond.

One area where children with ADHD often struggle is in school. It is not because they lack academic abilities, but rather because their "executive functioning" skills may be weak. Executive functioning refers to the self-regulating skills we all use in our daily lives, from organizing our time and materials to making decisions. By identifying and addressing these difficulties early on, we can provide the necessary support to help our children navigate the academic landscape more effectively.

ADHD can also affect a child's ability to control their emotions and learn from their past mistakes. They may struggle with understanding "cause and effect" or recognizing the consequences of their actions. Early intervention can help guide them in developing these essential skills, setting them on a path toward better emotional regulation and decision-making.

The first signs of ADHD often become apparent during the preschool years. By addressing behavior difficulties as soon as they arise, we effectively limit the negative impact of the disorder and prevent future impairments.

Here's why early diagnosis and intervention matter:

- **Understanding and Empathy:**

An early diagnosis provides a key to understanding your child's behavior and challenges. It helps unravel the mysteries behind their restlessness, impulsivity, or inattention. By recognizing ADHD as a potential factor, you gain a deeper understanding of their unique brain wiring and can approach their struggles with empathy, patience, and support.

- **Access to Resources and Support:**

Early diagnosis opens doors to a world of resources and support systems tailored to address ADHD challenges. From specialized educational programs to therapy and parenting strategies, you can tap into a range of interventions that can make a significant impact on your child's development. Timely access to these resources ensures they receive the support they need to thrive academically, socially, and emotionally.

- **Academic Success:**

Imagine your child as an eager student, thirsting for knowledge but struggling to keep up with the demands of the classroom. Early intervention for ADHD can help address academic challenges head-on. With targeted strategies, accommodations, and a supportive learning environment, your child can develop effective study skills, improve their focus, and achieve their true academic potential.

- **Social and Emotional Well-being:**

Navigating the social jungle can be particularly challenging for boys with ADHD. They may face difficulties in forming and maintaining friendships, managing emotions, and controlling impulsive behaviors. Early intervention equips them with the necessary tools to improve their social skills, self-regulation, and overall emotional well-being. By addressing these challenges early on, you can empower your child to build meaningful connections and navigate the complexities of social interactions.

- **Building Self-esteem and Resilience:**

Imagine your child as a brave adventurer facing obstacles in the jungle. Early intervention can help boost their self-esteem and resilience. By providing the right support, you can nurture their strengths, celebrate their achievements, and help them develop coping strategies to overcome challenges. This sets them on a path of self-discovery, confidence, and resilience that will benefit them throughout their lives.

Remember, as a parent, you are the compass guiding your child through their ADHD journey. Seeking an early diagnosis and intervening promptly can provide them with the tools and support they need to flourish in their unique way. Embrace this opportunity to embark on a proactive path, armed with knowledge, love, and understanding.

# Chapter 2

# Managing Behavior in Boys with ADHD

In this chapter, we will embark on an epic quest to conquer the challenges that come with parenting our spirited adventurers. Together, we will discover the secrets to fostering positive behavior while preserving their vibrant spirit. So, gather your strength, sharpen your wit, and get ready to unleash the power of effective behavior management!

## Effective discipline strategies for Boys with ADHD

When it comes to our spirited boys, effective discipline strategies can sometimes feel like taming a wild beast. But fear not, for I am here to guide you through the jungle of discipline.

Let us delve into some tried-and-true strategies that can help you maintain peace and harmony while fostering positive behavior:

**1. The Power of Consistency:**

Consistency is like the sturdy vines that keep us on track in the jungle of discipline. Establish clear rules and expectations, and stick to them like an intrepid explorer never straying from their path. Imagine the relief your child feels when they have a consistent set of rules to follow. They no longer need to guess what is right or wrong, as you have established a clear path for them to follow. This predictability is particularly crucial for children with ADHD, who often struggle with impulsivity and regulating their behaviors. By consistently reinforcing boundaries, you help them develop a sense of self-control and promote positive behavior.

When children with ADHD know what to expect, they feel a sense of security and stability. They can anticipate the consequences of their actions, which empowers them to make better choices. Consistency provides them with a reliable roadmap, making it easier for them to navigate the often-confusing landscape of their own impulses and behaviors.

Consistency also plays a vital role in building trust between you and your child. When they see that you consistently follow through on your promises, they learn that your words hold weight. This trust forms the foundation of a strong parent-child relationship, fostering open communication and cooperation.

Of course, we understand that consistency can be challenging amidst the unpredictable nature of parenting. There may be days when fatigue, stress, or other factors tempt you to stray from the established rules. But remember that consistency is not about being perfect; it is about making a sincere effort to maintain the boundaries you've set.

When you falter, take a deep breath, and reassess. Reflect on the importance of consistency for your child's growth and well-being. Rally your strength and recommit to the path you have chosen. Seek support from your partner, family, or friends who understand the unique challenges of parenting a child with ADHD.

## 2. The Art of Communication:

Communication is the secret language of the jungle, allowing you to connect with your child on a deeper level. Take the time to explain the reasons behind your expectations and the consequences of their actions. Use simple language and visuals to help them understand. Remember, open and respectful communication is the key to building trust and fostering cooperation. Let us delve deeper into this art form and unlock its potential to connect with your child on a deeper level.

When communicating with your child, keep in mind that simplicity is key. ADHD can make it challenging for children to process complex information or lengthy explanations. Use clear and concise language, breaking down concepts into smaller, digestible pieces. Visual aids, such as charts, diagrams, or even gestures, can enhance understanding and engagement.

Communication goes beyond just words. Non-verbal cues, such as facial expressions, tone of voice, and body language, convey powerful messages. Be mindful of your own non-verbal communication, ensuring that it aligns with the message you want to convey. A warm smile, gentle touch, or attentive posture can speak volumes and make your child feel valued and understood.

Remember that communication is a two-way street, so it is equally important to listen attentively to your child. Create a safe space where they feel comfortable sharing their thoughts, feelings, and concerns. By actively listening, you validate their experiences and show that their voice matters. This fosters a sense of mutual respect and strengthens your bond.

Imagine the joy and relief your child feels when they truly comprehend the expectations you've set. By communicating effectively, you empower them to make informed choices and take ownership of their actions. This builds their self-confidence and helps them develop crucial decision-making skills.

In the wilderness of communication, trust is the foundation upon which connections are built. When you engage in open and respectful dialogue with your child, you create an environment of trust and safety. This encourages them to be open and honest with you, fostering a deeper understanding of their needs and experiences.

## 3. The Magic of Positive Reinforcement:

Positive reinforcement is like discovering a hidden treasure in the depths of the jungle. Catch your child exhibiting good behavior and shower them with praise, encouragement, and rewards. Acknowledge their efforts, no matter how small, and watch their confidence soar. Remember, the more you focus on the positive, the more it will flourish.

Positive reinforcement works wonders because it emphasizes what your child is doing right. By focusing on their strengths and successes, you create a positive cycle that encourages them to continue displaying desirable behaviors. Like a growing plant nourished by sunlight and water, their confidence and self-esteem will flourish under the warmth of your recognition.

Imagine the joy and excitement in your child's eyes when they receive genuine praise from you. Your words become the fuel that propels them forward, motivating them to reach new heights. They feel seen, valued, and appreciated, which bolsters their belief in their own abilities. This newfound confidence can empower them to overcome challenges and persist in their efforts.

But the magic doesn't stop at verbal praise alone. Like a generous explorer bestowing treasures upon their loyal companion, consider incorporating tangible rewards as well. These rewards can be simple, yet meaningful, such as stickers, small treats, or special privileges. Choose rewards that align with your child's interests and preferences, ensuring they hold significant value in their eyes.

While positive reinforcement is a powerful tool, it is important to strike a balance. Offer praise and rewards genuinely and selectively, focusing on behavior that truly deserves recognition. This helps your child differentiate between what is genuinely praiseworthy and what is expected as part of their regular responsibilities.

## 4. The Compassionate Approach:

When it comes to discipline, empathy is your trusty compass, guiding you through the thickest of jungles. Imagine yourself walking in your child's shoes, seeing the world through their eyes. As you delve into their perspective, you gain insight into the unique challenges they face. Whether it is struggling with impulsivity, difficulty concentrating, or managing their emotions, understanding their experiences is crucial in guiding your response.

Instead of reacting with anger or frustration, the compassionate approach invites you to respond with empathy and kindness. Just as a gentle breeze soothes the sweltering heat of the jungle, your compassionate response can calm the storm of challenging behaviors. Take a moment to pause and remind yourself that your child's actions are often driven by underlying needs and struggles.

By adopting a compassionate mindset, you create a safe and supportive environment for your child to express themselves. You become a pillar of strength, offering understanding and acceptance rather than harsh judgment. This allows you to address the root causes of their behavior and work together towards meaningful solutions.

5. **The Power of Natural Consequences:**

Just as the jungle has its own set of natural consequences, so too can you use them to your advantage. When your child makes a mistake, allow them to experience the natural outcome of their actions. This helps them understand the cause-and-effect relationship and learn from their own experiences.

Natural consequences help your child understand the direct relationship between their choices and the outcomes they experience. Just as a wayward explorer who encounters a slippery path learns the importance of caution, your child can learn valuable life lessons by experiencing the natural consequences of their actions. This empowers them to make informed decisions and take responsibility for their choices.

It is important to note that the goal of natural consequences is not to punish your child but rather to guide them in understanding the impact of their behavior. By allowing them to face the natural outcomes, you provide an opportunity for growth and self-reflection. Through these experiences, they can develop a deeper understanding of cause and effect, learning from their own mistakes in a meaningful way.

For example, if your child consistently forgets to pack their lunch for school, a natural consequence may be going hungry until the next mealtime. This allows them to realize the importance of planning and taking responsibility for their own needs. Similarly, if they repeatedly procrastinate on completing their homework, a natural consequence may be receiving a lower grade or missing out on preferred activities due to unfinished work.

However, it is essential to consider the safety and well-being of your child when implementing natural consequences. In situations where their actions may pose a significant risk, it is crucial to intervene and provide guidance to ensure their safety.

## 6. The Strength of Structure:

In the chaos of the jungle, structure becomes your steadfast ally. Establish routines and schedules that provide a sense of order and predictability. Create a calm and organized environment to help your child focus and thrive. Structure acts as a guiding force, helping them stay on track and manage their impulsive tendencies.

Routines offer a familiar path in life, providing a comforting rhythm to your child's day. From morning routines to bedtime rituals, each structured activity becomes a stepping stone toward a more organized and purposeful life. This predictability helps your child feel more secure, reducing anxiety and creating a sense of stability.

Consider the benefits of a structured environment. Just as a sturdy tree provides a place to rest and gather strength, a calm, and organized space helps your child focus and thrive. Minimizing clutter and creating clear physical boundaries can reduce distractions and promote better concentration. This is especially important for children with ADHD, who may struggle with impulsivity and have difficulty staying on task.

Structure also plays a vital role in managing impulsive tendencies. Like a well-marked trail in the jungle, it guides your child, reminding them of expectations and providing gentle reminders to pause and think before acting. By incorporating visual cues, such as visual schedules or checklists, you can help your child navigate daily tasks and stay on track.

Remember, structure is not about rigid control or stifling creativity. It is about providing a supportive framework that allows your child to flourish. Flexibility within structure is key, allowing for adaptations and adjustments as needed. The goal is to strike a balance between predictability and spontaneity, nurturing your child's sense of autonomy while still providing the necessary guidance.

As you establish and maintain structure, involve your child in the process. Just as a skilled explorer collaborates with their team, invite your child to contribute to creating routines and schedules. This empowers them and fosters a sense of ownership, increasing their engagement and cooperation.

# Techniques for managing impulsive and hyperactive behavior

As parents, we know all too well the energy and enthusiasm that fills our childs days. While their zest for life is truly remarkable, it can sometimes present its own set of challenges. But fear not, dear parents! Let us embark on a journey together and explore some practical techniques to help manage impulsive and hyperactive behavior in our boys with ADHD.

- **Channel the Energy:**

Our boys are like little bundles of lightning, buzzing with boundless energy. One effective technique is to provide them with plenty of opportunities for physical activity. Engage them in sports, outdoor play, or even structured exercises. This not only helps them burn off excess energy but also promotes better focus and concentration. Think of it as giving them a designated outlet for their natural exuberance.

- **Create a Structured Routine:**

Establishing a predictable routine can work wonders in managing impulsive behavior. When your child knows what to expect it helps them navigate their day with greater ease. Set clear schedules for activities, including mealtimes, homework,

Managing Behavior in Boys with ADHD

playtime, and bedtime. Visual cues, such as charts or timers, can be helpful reminders and keep them on track.

- **Break Tasks into Manageable Chunks:**

The jungle of tasks can feel overwhelming for our boys with ADHD. Breaking larger tasks into smaller, more manageable chunks can make them less daunting. Encourage your child to focus on one step at a time, providing praise and encouragement along the way. Celebrate small victories to boost their confidence and motivation.

- **Use Visual Supports:**

Visual aids can be powerful allies in managing impulsivity and hyperactivity. Consider using visual schedules, charts, or checklists to help your child understand and remember what they need to do. Visual cues act as gentle reminders, offering a clear roadmap to follow. They can also help your child develop a sense of ownership and independence in managing their tasks.

- **Teach Self-Regulation Techniques:**

Helping our boys develop self-regulation skills is like giving them a compass in the jungle of emotions. Teach them techniques such as deep breathing, mindfulness, or counting to ten. These strategies provide a pause button, allowing them to take a moment and make more thoughtful choices when faced with impulsive urges.

- **Create a Calm and Organized Environment:**

A clutter-free and organized space can do wonders in minimizing distractions and promoting better focus. Designate specific areas for different activities, such as a quiet space for reading or a well-organized study area. Reduce visual and auditory distractions as much as possible to create an environment conducive to concentration.

- **Encourage Breaks and Rewards:**

Everyone needs a break from time to time, especially our boys who may find it challenging to sustain attention for extended periods. Incorporate regular short breaks during tasks or activities, allowing them to recharge and refocus. And don't forget to sprinkle in rewards! Recognize their efforts and achievements with praise, small treats, or special privileges. Positive reinforcement goes a long way in motivating and encouraging desired behaviors.

Remember, super-hero parents, managing impulsive and hyperactive behavior takes time and patience. Each child is unique, and what works for one may not work for another. Be open to trying different techniques and adapt them to suit your child's needs. Embrace the adventure, celebrate progress, and trust in your ability to guide your boys through the jungle of ADHD.

# The Role of Medication in Managing ADHD Symptoms

Let us dive into the intriguing subject of managing ADHD symptoms, where we will look at the role of medication as a helpful tool in our parenting toolbox. Ah, medication—the subject that occasionally makes us feel as though we are stumbling through a maze of queries and worries.

First and foremost, it is critical to keep in mind that medication is not a quick fix for all the problems connected to ADHD. Instead, it is a component of a bigger picture that helps manage symptoms and promotes the well-being of our kids. Consider it a solid compass that can guide you through the ups and downs of your adventure with ADHD.

The primary signs and symptoms of ADHD, such as impulsivity, hyperactivity, and inattention, can be significantly improved with medication. It functions by changing the neurotransmitter balance in the brain, enhancing executive function, and improving focus and self-control.

It is critical to keep an open mind while discussing medication with healthcare providers, especially those with experience in ADHD. They can offer helpful advice, evaluate your child's unique needs, and decide whether medication is the best course of action. Because every child is different, what works for one child might not work for another. You can decide whether or not medicine is the best option for your child with the help of your medical team.

It is also critical to understand that medicine is frequently used with other approaches and interventions. It can support other treatments for ADHD, such as behavioral therapies, counseling, and educational support. We can give our kids the most effective and well-rounded support system by combining a variety of techniques.

It is natural to be worried about possible medication side effects. Medication does have its own set of considerations, just like any other intervention. However, healthcare professionals carefully monitor its use and adjust dosages as needed. Regular check-ins and open communication with your child's healthcare team are key to ensuring that any side effects are addressed and managed effectively.

Remember, dear parents, the decision to try medication is a

personal one that should be made in partnership with healthcare professionals and based on your child's individual needs. It is important to be well-informed, ask questions, and seek support from trusted sources.

Lastly, always remember that medication is just one piece of the puzzle. It does not replace the love, support, and understanding we provide as parents. Our role remains essential in creating a nurturing environment, setting clear expectations, and teaching our children valuable skills to thrive in the world.

## Chapter 3

# Improving School Performance in Boys with ADHD

ADHD and school - two things that seem to endlessly clash. In this chapter, we will set our sights on improving the academic performance of our energetic boys with ADHD.

Boys with ADHD often face unique challenges in the classroom. Their restless minds and boundless energy can make it difficult for them to maintain attention, stay organized, and complete homework assignments. But fret not, for with the right tools and techniques, we can help guide them toward success.

In this chapter, we will delve into the common academic hurdles our boys may encounter. We will shine a light on their attention struggles and offer strategies to help them stay focused in the bustling classroom environment. From providing visual cues and seating arrangements to incorporating movement breaks and engaging activities, we will explore a variety of tactics to captivate their wandering minds.

But the journey doesn't end there! We will also venture into the depths of homework woes and reveal the secrets to conquering this formidable challenge. We will discuss effective strategies for organizing assignments, managing time, and creating a conducive homework routine. With a dash of structure, a sprinkle of motivation, and a pinch of parental involvement, we will transform homework time from a daunting task into a manageable adventure.

## Common academic challenges

In the dense foliage of the academic world, boys with ADHD may encounter some common challenges that can make their educational journey difficult. Understanding these hurdles is the first step in finding effective strategies to overcome them and set our boys up for success.

- **Difficulty in sustaining attention**

Let us take a closer look at the fascinating world of sustaining attention for boys with ADHD. Attention is like a precious gem, and for boys with ADHD, it can sometimes be a bit more challenging to keep that gem shining bright.

Imagine their minds as curious explorers, constantly seeking new sights and sounds in the jungle of information. They are eager to absorb everything around them, but their attention can be like a mischievous monkey, swinging from one thing to another.

**It is**

In a super busy classroom with its array of sights, sounds, and activities, distractions lurk at every turn. These distractions can be as captivating as a colorful bird or as noisy as a roaring waterfall. For boys with ADHD, it can be challenging to filter out these distractions and maintain their attention on the task at hand.

This difficulty in sustaining attention can impact their ability to absorb and process information effectively. It can also affect their performance on tasks that require sustained focus, such as reading, listening to instructions, or completing assignments. They may struggle to stay engaged during lectures, lose track of important details, or become easily bored or restless.

- **Issues with organization**

Organization is like a map that helps us navigate the complexities of daily life. It involves keeping track of belongings, managing time, and staying on top of responsibilities. However, for boys with ADHD, organization can feel like trying to untangle a thorny vine in the dense undergrowth.

One of the primary difficulties they may encounter is maintaining an organized physical space. Their backpacks, desks, and rooms can resemble a wild and untamed forest, with papers, books, and toys scattered everywhere. It can be a challenge for them to find what they need when they need it, causing frustration and wasting precious time.

Time management is another area where boys with ADHD may struggle. It is like trying to navigate the jungle without a compass, as they may have difficulty estimating the time required for tasks or prioritizing their activities. They may become easily distracted or lose track of time, resulting in missed deadlines or rushing to complete assignments at the last minute.

Planning and initiating tasks can be like forging a path through dense foliage. Boys with ADHD may find it challenging to break down larger tasks into smaller, manageable steps. They may procrastinate or feel overwhelmed by the sheer volume of work ahead, making it difficult to get started.

These organizational difficulties can impact their academic

performance, social interactions, and overall sense of well-being. They may feel disorganized, stressed, and struggle to meet expectations.

- **Problems in Completing homework assignments**

For boys with ADHD, completing assignments can sometimes feel like trekking through a dense jungle filled with challenges and distractions.

Boys with ADHD have minds that are always brimming with energy and excitement. When it comes to homework, though, their focus can be as elusive as a hidden treasure deep within the jungle. It is not that they don't want to complete their assignments, but rather that their attention can be easily captured by the calls of adventure that surround them.

One of the main challenges, as I mentioned previously as well, is sustaining focus and avoiding the siren calls of distractions. Boys with ADHD may find it difficult to resist the allure of video games, toys, or simply daydreaming about their next exciting escapade, and in all of this excitement, homework often takes the backseat.

Another obstacle they may encounter is managing their time effectively when completing assignments. Boys with ADHD may struggle with prioritizing their assignments or estimating how much time each task will take. They might get caught up in perfecting one aspect of their work, inadvertently leaving little time for other subjects.

Organizing their thoughts and homework materials can be another hurdle. It is like trying to gather the right equipment for a jungle expedition, but constantly misplacing a compass or forgetting a crucial tool. Boys with ADHD may have difficulty keeping their materials organized, finding necessary resources, or following instructions due to their impulsive nature or a tendency to get easily overwhelmed.

- **Difficulty in regulating emotions in the classroom**

In the bustling classroom, filled with a variety of activities, interactions, and academic demands, it can be like trying to balance on a tightrope for our boys with ADHD. Regulating emotions can feel like taming an animal that loves to swing from high to low branches, making it challenging to maintain a sense of calm.

One of the key difficulties they may face is managing their impulsivity. Boys with ADHD may tend to act before thinking, blurting out answers, or interrupting others, driven by their vibrant energy and enthusiasm.

Another challenge they may encounter is coping with frustration and setbacks Boys with ADHD may become easily overwhelmed when faced with difficult tasks or when things do not go as planned. This can lead to frustration, outbursts of emotions, or even giving up altogether.

Additionally, maintaining emotional self-regulation in the face of distractions can be like trying to stay focused while a parade of animals passes by. Boys with ADHD may find it challenging to ignore external stimuli, such as noise or visual distractions, which can break their emotional balance and make it harder to concentrate on the tasks at hand

- **Hyper-activity and Restlessness**

In the classroom, where sitting still and staying focused are the expected norms, it can be like trying to contain a cheetah within four walls. Hyperactivity is like a powerful river rushing through their veins, constantly propelling them forward. They may feel the need to move their bodies, tap their feet, or squirm in their seats. Sitting quietly may feel extremely uncomfortable and challenging for them.

Restlessness is another part of their energetic nature. Boys with ADHD may struggle with maintaining attention, frequently shifting their focus from one thing to another, like a curious explorer drawn to every fascinating sight in the jungle.

Understanding these challenges allows us to devise effective strategies to support our boys academically. By providing tailored solutions and implementing a supportive framework, we can help them navigate the academic jungle with greater ease. In the upcoming sections, we will explore practical tips and techniques to address these challenges head-on and empower our boys to flourish in their educational pursuits. Remember, we're in this together, and with the right tools, our boys can conquer the academic world and reach new heights of success.

# Strategies for improving attention and focus in the classroom

Now that we have established that the classroom is akin to a jungle and that distractions come from every which way, it is time to dive into the vast array of strategies available to help our boys deal with said distractions. While there is no one size fits all solution to a lack of focus and attention, these strategies can still benefit most boys with ADHD.

- **Organization and Structure**

One effective strategy is to create a structured and organized environment. It is like carving a clear path through the jungle, removing any unnecessary distractions. Boys with ADHD benefit from having a designated workspace, free from clutter and visual disturbances.

By providing a clear agenda or schedule for the day, we hand them a compass to navigate the jungle of time management. Having a visual representation of what lies ahead allows them to mentally prepare and understand the flow of the day

Within this structured environment, we can also introduce organizational strategies that act as tools to tame the wild undergrowth of disorganization. For instance, using color-coded folders or binders for different subjects helps boys with ADHD keep their materials in order.

Additionally, visual cues and reminders can be like helpful signposts along their journey. Placing visual prompts, such as checklists or sticky notes, in their workspace or on their desk serves as gentle reminders of important tasks or steps to follow. These cues act as guideposts, keeping them on the right path and reducing the chances of getting lost in the jungle of distractions.

By establishing a structured and organized environment, we provide boys with ADHD with the tools they need to navigate the classroom jungle with greater ease. With clear paths, designated spaces, and visual cues, we create a space where they can focus their attention, manage their materials, and stay on track. By removing unnecessary distractions and providing a roadmap for success, we empower them to confidently explore the jungle of learning and thrive academically.

- **Bite-size information**

Breaking tasks into smaller, manageable chunks is another valuable approach. By breaking tasks into manageable chunks, we transform the daunting jungle of assignments into an exciting adventure. We empower boys with ADHD to approach their work with confidence, knowing that they can conquer one step at a time. Through this approach, they gain a sense of control, build resilience, and develop valuable skills in time management and task completion.

Clear instructions are essential when presenting these smaller tasks. Just as a skilled guide provides precise directions, we provide boys with ADHD with explicit instructions and expectations for each segment of the task. This clarity helps them focus their attention and understand what is required of them. It is like having a compass that points them in the right direction, keeping them on track and preventing them from getting lost in the vast wilderness of the assignment.

As they complete each smaller task, boys with ADHD experience small victories and successes. It is like discovering hidden treasures along the journey, boosting their confidence and motivation. These mini-accomplishments act as milestones, reminding them of their progress and fueling their determination to continue moving forward.

- **Visual Aids & Interactive elements**

Incorporating visual aids and interactive methods can also enhance their attention and engagement. Visual cues act as our guiding compass, helping us navigate through the jungle of information and concepts. For boys with ADHD, who may struggle with sustaining attention, these visual aids become powerful tools that capture their interest and enhance their understanding. It is like discovering a treasure trove of knowledge presented in a way that speaks directly to their curious minds.

Charts, diagrams, and infographics are like colorful snapshots, showcasing key information in a visually appealing manner. These visual aids break down complex ideas into bite-sized pieces, making them easier to digest and comprehend. It is as if we're handing them a pair of binoculars to zoom in on the intricate details of the jungle, allowing them to explore and absorb information with greater clarity.

Hands-on activities take the adventure a step further, inviting boys with ADHD to actively participate and engage with their learning By incorporating interactive methods, such as experiments, role-playing, or group projects, we tap into their natural curiosity and provide a multi-sensory experience. This active involvement keeps their minds and bodies engaged, preventing restlessness, and increasing their ability to sustain attention.

When visual aids and interactive methods are utilized, the classroom becomes an immersive pool of learning. Boys with ADHD are captivated by the vibrant visuals, eager to explore, and actively participate in their education. These strategies create an environment where information comes alive, and concepts become more tangible and relatable.

- **Incorporating movement and physical activity**

Another valuable technique is incorporating movement and physical activity. Boys with ADHD may benefit from short breaks for stretching or engaging in physical activities that allow them to release excess energy and improve their ability to focus.

Boys with ADHD are like spirited explorers, brimming with energy that often seems boundless. Sitting still for extended periods can feel like being trapped in a cage for these young adventurers. That's why incorporating movement and physical activity into their learning environment is like setting their spirits free to roam and explore the vast jungle of knowledge.

Short breaks for stretching, jumping, or engaging in physical activities act as vital rest stops along their academic journey. It is like discovering a hidden oasis in the midst of the jungle, offering a much-needed opportunity for boys with ADHD to release excess energy and rejuvenate their minds. These breaks serve as a release valve, allowing them to reset and recharge, which in turn enhances their ability to focus on tasks at hand.

Engaging in physical activities also provides a valuable outlet for their restlessness and hyperactivity. Whether it is playing a quick game of catch, doing a few yoga poses, or participating in a short exercise routine, these activities allow them to expend energy in a constructive and beneficial way.

Incorporating movement and physical activity has a profound impact on their ability to focus and maintain attention. As they engage in physical movement, their brain releases neurotransmitters that promote alertness and improve their ability to concentrate. They become more primed and ready to dive into learning, just like an explorer bracing themselves for the wonders of the jungle.

- **Using Technology**

In today's digital age, technology has become an integral part of our lives, and it can also be a valuable asset in the classroom. Educational apps, interactive learning platforms, and digital organizers act as a digital arsenal, empowering boys with ADHD to embark on their educational journey with confidence and excitement.

Educational apps are like hidden treasures buried deep within the jungle. They offer a vast array of interactive and engaging learning experiences, tailored to capture the interest of young minds. From math and science to language arts and critical thinking, these apps transform traditional learning into an exciting adventure. Boys with ADHD can explore concepts, solve puzzles, and participate in interactive activities that make learning come alive. These apps provide a level of interactivity and immediate feedback that fosters engagement and encourages active participation.

Interactive learning platforms are like virtual expeditions through the vast world of knowledge. They provide a digital landscape where boys with ADHD can explore, collaborate, and learn at their own pace. These platforms offer multimedia resources, interactive lessons, and opportunities for online discussions and collaborations. By incorporating technology into their education, we provide them with a platform that meets them where they are, catering to their preferences for visual and interactive learning experiences.

Digital organizers act as their personal jungle guides, keeping them on track and organized. These tools help boys with ADHD manage their assignments, deadlines, and schedules in a digital format. With reminders, task lists, and calendar features, digital organizers provide structure and support. They offer a visual representation of their responsibilities, breaking them down into manageable chunks. By leveraging technology, we assist them in developing essential organizational skills that are key to academic success.

Technology serves as a bridge, connecting boys with ADHD to a world of endless possibilities and opportunities for growth. By integrating educational apps, interactive learning platforms, and digital organizers, we tap into their innate curiosity and provide them with tools to actively participate in their learning journey.

- **Fostering a positive and supportive learning environment**

Lastly, fostering a positive and supportive learning environment is crucial. Encouraging collaboration, celebrating individual achievements, and providing praise and recognition can boost their motivation and help them maintain their focus.

Remember, with the right strategies and support, boys with ADHD can develop their attention and focus skills, transforming the classroom jungle into a place of discovery and growth. So, let us embark on this journey together, equipping them with the tools they need to flourish in the realm of learning.

## 8 Tips for organizing and completing homework assignments

Ah, the mighty homework assignments! They can sometimes feel like an untamed beast lurking in the depths of the jungle, especially for boys with ADHD. But fear not, with a few handy tips and tricks, we can conquer these tasks and turn them into manageable adventures. So, grab your backpack, and let us embark on our quest to organize and complete homework assignments with style!

**Tip 1:** Establish a Homework Routine - Like a seasoned explorer, create a consistent homework routine that becomes second nature for your child. Set aside a specific time and place for homework, free from distractions. Whether it is a cozy corner of the living room or a designated study area, make it a special homework zone. By establishing a routine, you provide structure and a signal to your child's brain that it is time to focus and get to work.

**Tip 2:** Break it Down - Remember, we don't want to tackle the entire jungle in one leap. Break down homework assignments into smaller, manageable tasks. Help your child create a to-do list or use a planner to prioritize and organize their assignments. By breaking it down, you make the workload feel less overwhelming and allow for a sense of accomplishment with each completed task.

**Tip 3:** Clear the Path - Just as a jungle explorer clears away overgrown vines, help your child clear away any unnecessary distractions. Create a clutter-free and organized workspace where they can concentrate. Remove tempting gadgets or toys that might divert their attention. Encourage them to focus solely on the task at hand, like a true homework hero.

**Tip 4:** Time Management - Time can be a slippery creature, but we can tame it! Teach your child time management skills by using visual cues and timers. Set realistic time limits for each task and use a timer to help them stay on track. Encourage breaks in between assignments to recharge their energy. By mastering time management, they can make the most of their homework adventures.

**Tip 5:** Find other parents with children with ADHD- Remember, you don't have to navigate this jungle alone. Reach out to other parents who have gone through, or are going through similar experiences as you. You could exchange helpful tricks, discuss life as a parent of neurodivergent kids, or even just rant when you're frustrated.

**Tip 6:** Celebrate Milestones - In the jungle, even the smallest victories are worth celebrating. Acknowledge and celebrate your child's efforts and achievements along the way. Offer praise, rewards, or special treats as a way to motivate and encourage them. Positive reinforcement is a powerful tool that fuels their motivation and builds their confidence.

**Tip 7:** Take Breaks - Remember, even jungle explorers need breaks to recharge and refuel. Encourage your child to take short breaks during homework sessions. They can stretch, have a healthy snack, or engage in a quick physical activity to release pent-up energy. These breaks rejuvenate their focus and help them return to their tasks with renewed energy.

**Tip 8**: Seek Help When Needed - If your child is struggling with a particular subject or concept, don't hesitate to seek additional help. Reach out to their teachers or consider hiring a tutor who specializes in supporting children with ADHD. Remember, seeking help is a sign of strength and dedication to their academic success.

With these tips in your arsenal, you are well-prepared to conquer the homework jungle alongside your child with ADHD. Remember, every adventure has its challenges, but with patience, perseverance, and a sprinkle of fun, you can transform homework time into a rewarding and enjoyable experience.

## Chapter 4

# Teaching Social Skills to Boys with ADHD

As parents, we understand that the social landscape can sometimes feel like a wild terrain, especially for our boys with ADHD. But fear not! This chapter is here to arm you with powerful techniques and strategies that will transform your social journey into a thrilling adventure.

In this corner of the jungle, we will uncover the common social challenges that our boys with ADHD may encounter. Making friends might seem as treacherous as crossing a crocodile-infested river. Reading social cues might feel like deciphering a hidden code. And managing emotions can sometimes feel like taming a wild beast within. But worry not, intrepid explorers! We have the tools and knowledge to conquer these challenges.

Throughout this chapter, we will dive deep into the art of teaching communication and social interaction skills. We will discover practical techniques for fostering friendships, decoding social cues, and embracing emotional intelligence. We will navigate the winding paths of self-esteem and build bridges of positive relationships.

But remember, in this adventure, there are no wrong turns or dead ends. Each step forward, no matter how small, brings us closer to our goal. So, put on your social explorer hat, dust off your listening ears, and get ready to embark on an unforgettable journey into the heart of social skills education.

# Common social challenges for boys with ADHD

In the dense jungle of social interactions, boys with ADHD may encounter a few unique challenges along the way. As we navigate this terrain, let us shine a light on some of the common social hurdles they may face. Remember, understanding these challenges is the first step towards overcoming them and guiding our young adventurers to success.

- **Making Friends**

In the wild world of friendship, boys with ADHD may find themselves on a daring quest to make new connections. Think of it as embarking on a thrilling adventure through uncharted territory. But just like any brave explorer, they may face some unique challenges along the way.

Initiating conversations can sometimes feel like deciphering an ancient code. The moment to approach a potential friend arrives, and their mind races with questions like, "What should I say? Will they find me interesting? Did I remember to brush my teeth?" It is like trying to navigate a treacherous path while balancing on a tightrope.

And let us not forget the exhilarating group activities. From team sports to school projects, the fast-paced nature of social interactions can feel like a wild roller coaster ride. Boys with ADHD may struggle to keep up, sometimes feeling overwhelmed by the flurry of activity around them. It is like being caught in a whirlwind, trying to catch their breath while everyone else seems to effortlessly blend in.

- **Reading Social Cues**

In the vibrant jungle of social interactions, non-verbal cues are like the colorful feathers of exotic birds, guiding us through the dense foliage of communication. But for our adventurous boys with ADHD, decoding these signals can sometimes feel like attempting to decipher a secret language.

Imagine the scene: a group of friends huddled together, their faces a canvas of expressions. While others effortlessly read the hidden messages in their raised eyebrows, playful smirks, or even the occasional eye roll, our brave boys may find themselves lost in translation. It is like trying to understand a monkey's chatter without speaking their language.

Body language, too, holds the key to this intricate puzzle of social cues. While some navigate the dance of conversation with graceful gestures and postures, our boys may feel like they are performing an impromptu dance routine without knowing the steps. It is like being caught in a wild tango, where every misstep can lead to confusion or even embarrassment.

And let us not forget the magical world of tone of voice. The way words are spoken can convey a spectrum of emotions, from excitement to disappointment, from sincerity to sarcasm. But for our intrepid explorers, distinguishing between these nuances can feel like searching for a hidden treasure in a vast, echoing cave. It is like trying to unravel the mysteries of a mystical language, where the same words can hold entirely different meanings depending on their intonation.

- **Managing Emotions**

Imagine our young adventurers in the social jungle, facing the daunting challenge of managing their emotions. It is like being handed a map written in an ancient language that they're still deciphering. They may stumble upon unexpected emotional swamps, where frustration and impatience lurk beneath the surface, ready to ensnare them.

Sometimes, it is as if their emotions play a game of hide-and-seek, camouflaging themselves in the dense foliage. They struggle to identify and understand what they're feeling, leaving them bewildered and uncertain. It is like trying to spot a hidden chameleon amidst a sea of vibrant leaves.

And oh, the intensity of those emotions! It is like a tropical storm rolling through the jungle, shaking the very foundation of their composure. Their emotions may bubble and brew, threatening to overflow like a cascading waterfall. It becomes a juggling act, trying to maintain balance while navigating the treacherous terrain of social interactions.

In the midst of this emotional jungle, our boys with ADHD may find it challenging to keep their reactions in check. It is like trying to tame a mischievous monkey swinging from branch to branch. The impulse to blurt out thoughts or lash out in frustration can be difficult to control, creating a whirlwind of chaos in their interactions.

- **Social Rules**

Picture our adventurous explorers venturing into the realm of social interactions, armed with their trusty map of unwritten rules. But oh, what a tangled web it can be! The social rulebook may seem like a mystical artifact written in disappearing ink, leaving our boys with ADHD scratching their heads in confusion.

It is like trying to navigate through a maze of invisible vines. They can't see the paths clearly laid out before them, and they may accidentally step on toes or bump into fellow explorers along the way. Taking turns becomes a daring dance, with a few missteps and accidental twirls thrown in for good measure. It is like trying to follow the beat of a jungle drum that keeps changing its rhythm.

And let us not forget about personal space – that elusive concept that seems to elude our intrepid adventurers. It is like wandering through a dense jungle without a machete, occasionally stumbling into someone's comfort zone. Oops! Sorry, fellow explorer, didn't mean to invade your territory. The struggle to understand the invisible boundaries of personal space can be a wild ride indeed.

Sharing is another challenge that often beckons our boys with ADHD to embark on an expedition of selflessness. It is like trying to divide a single piece of fruit among a group of hungry monkeys – a precarious balancing act. They may struggle to grasp the delicate art of compromise and find themselves unintentionally hoarding the bananas of friendship.

- **Perspective-Taking**

Perspective-taking is like decoding a mysterious language spoken only in the hidden corners of the social jungle. Boys with ADHD may find themselves facing the challenging task of unraveling the thoughts, feelings, and perspectives of others.

It is as if they are equipped with a pair of special spectacles, designed to provide them with a glimpse into the minds of their fellow explorers. But oh, what a challenge it can be to adjust the lenses just right! Sometimes, the spectacles might fog up, making it difficult to see beyond their own point of view. It is like trying to peer through a thick jungle mist, where everything appears hazy and unclear.

Empathy, that precious gem of connection, may feel like a rare treasure hidden deep within the dense undergrowth. Boys with ADHD may struggle to fully grasp the emotions and experiences of others, as if they are searching for a hidden oasis in a vast desert of social understanding.

Walking in someone else's shoes becomes a daring feat, like tiptoeing along a narrow, winding jungle path. They may stumble upon unexpected twists and turns, unsure of how to navigate the intricate web of emotions and perspectives that shape our human interactions.

- **Maintaining Conversations**

Maintaining conversations for boys with ADHD can be an exhilarating expedition through the social jungle. Picture this: you're swinging on vines of dialogue, trying to stay in sync with the rhythm of the conversation. But for boys with ADHD, the vines may sway and bend unpredictably as their minds embark on daring adventures.

Their attention may wander, just like jumping from branch to branch. They might enthusiastically share their latest obsession with dinosaurs one moment, only to switch gears and dive into the mysteries of outer space the next. It is like navigating through a vibrant canopy, where every topic is a new vine to explore.

Listening attentively can be like tracking elusive animals in the jungle. Boys with ADHD might find their minds captivated by the intriguing sights and sounds around them, causing their focus to dart from one point of interest to another. Staying on track in a conversation can feel as challenging as catching a quick glimpse of a rare creature before it disappears into the foliage.

Taking turns can be like balancing on a vine, carefully passing the conversational baton. Boys with ADHD may struggle to wait their turn, their excitement bubbling up like the calls of colorful birds. It is as if their enthusiasm propels them forward, and they cannot resist interjecting with their thoughts and ideas. Patience becomes an adventurous endeavor, like waiting for a timid jungle creature to reveal itself.

- **Transitioning Between Activities**

Transitioning between activities for boys with ADHD can be like navigating a thrilling obstacle course where timing is everything.

Moving from playtime to learning time requires a careful balance, just like jumping from a playful tree branch to a sturdy vine. Boys with ADHD might be captivated by the excitement of play, their imaginations running wild like mischievous monkeys. Asking them to shift gears can be like coaxing a curious creature to leave their favorite jungle hideout.

Similarly, transitioning between classroom activities can be an adventure in adaptability. It is like trekking through various landscapes, encountering different challenges along the way. Boys with ADHD may struggle to switch their focus and adapt to new tasks, their minds racing like a cheetah through tall grass. It is as if they need a gentle nudge, like the guidance of a wise jungle guide, to help them find their footing in this ever-changing environment.

- **Interpreting Sarcasm and Figurative Language**

Interpreting sarcasm and figurative language can feel like exploring the secret passages of the social undergrowth for boys with ADHD. It is like embarking on a quest to decipher hidden messages that are concealed within the leaves and branches of conversation.

For these boys, grasping the subtle nuances of sarcasm, metaphors, and figurative language can be as challenging as untangling a complex puzzle. It is like encountering a riddle that requires a keen eye and a touch of imagination to unravel its true meaning.

While others effortlessly navigate the winding path of figurative language, boys with ADHD may find themselves venturing down a more literal route. Like intrepid explorers armed with literal interpretations, they may miss the playful twists and turns that lie beneath the surface.

Imagine a conversation as a dense thicket of words, where hidden meanings lurk amidst the foliage. While others might detect the subtle cues and humorous undertones, boys with ADHD might find themselves entangled in the literal interpretation, unaware of the vibrant world of figurative language that dances around them.

# 6 Techniques for teaching communication and social interaction skills

As I mentioned before, teaching communication and social interaction skills to boys with ADHD is like equipping them with a compass and a guidebook for navigating the complex terrain of social interactions. By providing them with practical techniques and strategies, we can empower them to confidently explore the social jungle. Let us dive into some effective techniques that can make this journey both fun and enlightening:

1. **Role-playing Adventures:**

Role-playing adventures are like stepping into the shoes of fearless explorers in the social jungle. Boys with ADHD can unleash their imagination and embark on exciting quests where they can practice essential social skills in a safe and supportive environment. Let us delve deeper into this thrilling technique and discover how it can empower them to navigate social interactions with confidence.

Through role-playing activities, boys with ADHD can actively engage in social scenarios that mirror real-life situations. They can practice initiating conversations with peers, teachers, or even unfamiliar individuals they encounter on their jungle journey. By taking on different roles, they can explore different perspectives, learning to adapt their communication style to suit each unique encounter.

Imagine a brave adventurer initiating a conversation with a fellow explorer, asking questions about their favorite discoveries or sharing exciting stories from their own expeditions. They can experiment with different conversation starters, tone of voice, and body language, discovering the impact each has on the interaction. With each role-played conversation, they build confidence and hone their communication skills, equipping themselves with tools for successful social interactions.

Role-playing adventures also provide a platform for navigating conflicts and misunderstandings. Boys with ADHD can take on the challenging role of conflict resolution, exploring ways to express their thoughts and emotions effectively while considering the feelings of others. They can practice active listening, assertiveness, and compromise, all while embracing the spirit of adventure and collaboration.

As the adventurers immerse themselves in these role-playing scenarios, they sharpen their ability to read social cues. They learn to interpret body language, facial expressions, and subtle nuances in tone, like expert trackers deciphering signs left by elusive jungle creatures. This heightened awareness allows them to respond appropriately to social cues, fostering deeper connections and understanding with those around them.

Through these role-playing adventures, boys with ADHD develop a deeper understanding of different perspectives and the importance of empathy. They witness firsthand how their actions and words can impact others, inspiring them to approach social interactions with kindness and respect. They learn to step outside of their own perspective and explore the rich tapestry of human experiences, making connections that transcend the boundaries of their own jungle expedition.

Role-playing adventures bring an element of excitement and fun to social skills training. They allow boys with ADHD to unleash their creativity, building their communication skills while immersing themselves in thrilling and imaginative scenarios. With each adventure, they gain confidence, resilience, and a deeper understanding of the social landscape.

**2. Social Stories Safari:**

Social Stories Safari is a thrilling expedition through the realm of storytelling where boys with ADHD can discover the secrets of social interactions. Imagine setting off on a journey filled with vibrant tales that illuminate social challenges and unveil the keys to success. Get ready to explore the power of Social Stories Safari and witness how it transforms boys with ADHD into savvy navigators of the social jungle.

In this adventure, stories become our trusty compasses, leading us through the intricate paths of social situations. These tales, carefully crafted and personalized, bring to life the encounters and dilemmas that boys with ADHD may encounter in their everyday interactions. Through the magic of storytelling, we can delve into the rich tapestry of social experiences, exploring the nuances and complexities that lie within.

With Social Stories Safari, boys with ADHD can dive into narratives that highlight the intricacies of making friends, interpreting social cues, and managing emotions. They meet characters who encounter the same obstacles they do, facing them head-on with courage and resilience. These stories provide a mirror, reflecting their own experiences and offering guidance on how to navigate the social terrain.

As we read and discuss these stories, we embark on meaningful conversations that shed light on the underlying themes and lessons. We explore the thoughts and motivations of the characters, examining their actions and consequences. Together, we unravel the hidden treasures within the stories, decoding the subtle cues and unwritten rules that govern social interactions.

By engaging in the Social Stories Safari, boys with ADHD learn to connect the dots between the fictional world and their own experiences. They develop a deeper understanding of cause and effect, learning to anticipate the outcomes of their actions. Through discussions and reflections, they gain valuable insights into the perspectives and emotions of others, expanding their empathy and fostering meaningful connections.

The beauty of the Social Stories Safari is that it can be tailored to each adventurer's needs and experiences. Personalized stories can be created, incorporating specific challenges and triumphs that resonate with the individual. These personalized tales become cherished companions, offering guidance and support on their unique journey through the social jungle.

### 3. Team Up for Cooperative Games:

As boys with ADHD dive into the realm of cooperative play, they embark on thrilling adventures that unlock the secrets of effective social interaction. Imagine a team of eager explorers, ready to tackle challenges together, supporting one another every step of the way.

In this exciting journey, cooperative games become the heart and soul of our expedition. Whether it is gathering around a board game, participating in a sports activity, or engaging in a group project, these experiences offer a playground for honing essential social skills. Through these games, boys with ADHD can learn the art of cooperation, turn-taking, active listening, and effective communication.

Imagine a board game unfolding on a table, where every player is a valued member of the team. Each roll of the dice or strategic move presents an opportunity for boys with ADHD to practice waiting their turn, considering different perspectives, and collaborating with their fellow adventurers. In the process, they discover the joy of shared victories, as well as the resilience to face setbacks as a united front.

Cooperative games also extend beyond the tabletop and into the realm of sports and group projects. Picture a group of teammates on a soccer field, their efforts seamlessly coordinated as they work together towards a common goal. Boys with ADHD have the chance to experience the thrill of collaboration, as they communicate with their teammates, support one another, and adapt their strategies in real time.

Group projects offer yet another avenue for practicing teamwork and communication. As boys with ADHD work together on a shared assignment, they tap into their unique strengths and perspectives. Each contribution becomes a building block in the collective endeavor, fostering a sense of belonging and accomplishment. Through these collaborative efforts, they develop valuable skills in negotiation, compromise, and effective problem-solving.

Cooperative games create a safe and supportive environment where boys with ADHD can explore the intricacies of social interaction. They learn the importance of active listening, respecting diverse opinions, and working collaboratively towards a shared objective. By experiencing the joys and challenges of cooperative play, they develop empathy, teamwork, and effective communication skills that extend far beyond the game itself.

### 4. Encourage Empathy Expeditions:

Empathy expeditions are like immersive experiences that allow boys with ADHD to step into the shoes of others and truly comprehend their emotions. It is a quest that begins with simple yet powerful activities, where we ignite the flame of empathy and set it ablaze.

Imagine opening the pages of a book or gathering around a screen to witness the adventures of characters who journey through a myriad of emotions. These tales become windows into the human experience, providing opportunities to discuss and explore the feelings and motivations of the characters. Boys with ADHD can engage in lively discussions, sharing their own insights and reflections, as they develop the ability to relate to the emotional landscapes of others.

Personal experiences serve as useful compasses in this massive voyage, leading our explorers to a more profound comprehension of empathy. Encourage boys with ADHD to relate personal experiences that made them feel happy, unhappy, frustrated, or afraid. They create a connection and build empathy by bridging the gap between their own feelings and those of others via the power of storytelling.

But let us not lose sight of the importance of community and the wider influence we can have. Boys with ADHD have a special chance to explore their surroundings through empathy expeditions, taking part in community projects, donating their time, and providing a helping hand. They see personally how their deeds affect others when they perform acts of kindness. These encounters weave their own emotions into those of the people they meet, constructing a tapestry of empathy that fosters a strong sense of compassion and understanding.

Boys with ADHD who participate in empathy excursions learn how to navigate their emotions with ease and develop genuine empathy. They develop a good sense of observation and learn to pay attention to both spoken and nonverbal signs that disclose the needs and feelings of those around them. They acquire the skills necessary to function as bulwarks of empathy in a world that can sometimes feel overwhelming by learning to inquire, help, and offer comfort.

**5. The Art of Conversation:**

Ah, the art of conversation—a masterpiece waiting to be painted! For boys with ADHD, let us embark on a creative journey where we unravel the secrets of engaging and meaningful interactions. Imagine this adventure as a canvas, where brushstrokes of communication skills bring vibrant colors and captivating conversations to life.

First, let us begin with the basics—the foundation upon which the art of conversation is built. Just as an artist focuses on each brushstroke, we break down conversation into manageable steps. Boys with ADHD can start by mastering fundamental skills, like making eye contact and actively listening. These are the gentle strokes that create a solid connection with others.

As we progress, let us add layers of complexity to our conversational canvas. Practice becomes key here. Encourage boys with ADHD to engage in conversations about their interests or daily experiences. Whether it is discussing their favorite hobbies, sharing stories from their day, or exploring their imaginative worlds, these conversations lay the groundwork for building confidence and connection.

Now, let us introduce the art of asking open-ended questions—the bold brushstrokes that invite depth and discovery. Teach them the power of curiosity, encouraging them to inquire about others' thoughts, dreams, and experiences. By asking questions that cannot be answered with a simple "yes" or "no," they unlock the doors to engaging and meaningful conversations.

As our young conversational artists gain confidence, let us delve into the nuances of responding appropriately. This is where the artistry truly shines. Help them understand the importance of active listening, empathetic responses, and respectful communication. Like a skilled artist, they learn to choose their words wisely, adding just the right hues of understanding, support, and encouragement.

Throughout this artistic journey, remind boys with ADHD that conversations are not solo performances but duets where each participant takes turns. Teach them the dance of conversation—knowing when to step forward and share, and when to gracefully step back and listen. This harmony of taking turns allows for balanced and inclusive interactions, creating a symphony of connection.

As our young artists grow in their conversational prowess, let us encourage them to explore more complex social topics. Like venturing into uncharted artistic territories, they can engage in discussions about world events, literature, or thought-provoking ideas. These conversations become rich landscapes where their thoughts and perspectives intertwine with others', creating a masterpiece of intellectual exchange.

Remember, the art of conversation is not just about mastering skills, but also about cultivating genuine interest and connection. Encourage boys with ADHD to show curiosity and appreciation for the diverse perspectives and experiences of those around them. This genuine interest becomes the heart of their conversational masterpiece, radiating warmth and creating lasting connections.

## 6. Positive Reinforcement Expeditions:

For boys with ADHD, positive reinforcement becomes the compass that guides them on their social skills journey. Let us join them on these uplifting expeditions, where we recognize and celebrate their progress and successes, no matter how small.

Positive reinforcement acts as a powerful tool in their backpack, boosting their confidence and motivation. When they demonstrate effective communication skills, such as active listening, making eye contact, or using respectful language, let us acknowledge and celebrate their efforts. It is like shining a spotlight on their achievements, illuminating their path, and encouraging them to continue their remarkable journey.

But positive reinforcement is not just about the big victories. In the social jungle, even the tiniest steps forward deserve applause. When they take a deep breath before responding, navigate a difficult conversation with grace, or show empathy towards a friend in need, let us make sure they know how proud we are of their growth and resilience. Like expert explorers, they have mastered the art of adapting and learning from their experiences.

In these expeditions of positive reinforcement, let us create a culture of celebration and support. Along their journey, let us reward their progress with a variety of treasures: sincere praise, high-fives, special privileges, or even a fun outing. These rewards become the fuel that propels them forward, igniting their desire to continue exploring and refining their social skills.

As we cheer them on, let us also foster a sense of self-awareness and reflection. Encourage boys with ADHD to recognize and celebrate their own achievements. Like skilled trackers, they can observe their growth, identifying moments where their newfound communication strategies made a difference. These self-reflections become the cherished souvenirs of their progress, reminding them of their resilience and capacity for growth.

In these positive reinforcement expeditions, let us create a supportive community of fellow explorers. Engage family members, teachers, and peers in celebrating their milestones. Share stories of their social triumphs, allowing others to witness and appreciate their growth. This collective celebration not only uplifts them but also inspires others to embark on their own journeys of social skill development.

Remember, teaching communication and social interaction skills to boys with ADHD is a collaborative and ongoing adventure. By incorporating these techniques and infusing them with a sense of excitement and fun, we can empower them to navigate the social jungle with confidence, forming meaningful connections and building strong relationships along the way.

# Strategies for building self-esteem and positive relationships

Isn't it nice to picture a world where self-esteem flourishes like vibrant flowers in a meadow, and positive relationships bloom like strong and sturdy trees? Boys with ADHD deserve to thrive in this enchanting landscape, where their self-worth blossoms, and their connections with others are nourished. Let us dive into strategies to cultivate self-esteem and foster positive relationships in these remarkable boys. These strategies plus those that we have discussed earlier, will help you help your kid to make ADHD his strength, not weakness.

- **Unleash the Superpowers Within:**

Help boys with ADHD recognize and celebrate their unique strengths and abilities. Just like superheroes, they possess incredible qualities that make them special. Encourage them to explore their passions and talents, whether it is art, sports, music, or problem-solving. By discovering and nurturing their superpowers, they can build a strong foundation of self-esteem and embrace their true potential.

As they uncover their superpowers, be their biggest cheerleaders. Celebrate their accomplishments, no matter how small, and remind them of their incredible abilities. Just as superheroes use their powers to make a positive impact on the world, encourage them to use their talents to benefit others and make a difference. Whether it is creating artwork to brighten someone's day, using their sports skills to inspire their peers, sharing their musical talents to uplift spirits, or utilizing their problem-solving abilities to help friends overcome challenges, their superpowers have the potential to bring joy and positivity to those around them.

By nurturing their superpowers, we help them build a strong foundation of self-esteem. They realize that their unique abilities make them special and valuable. Embracing their true potential, they gain confidence and a sense of purpose. They become the heroes of their own stories, equipped with the skills and strengths to navigate the challenges that lie ahead.

- **Encourage a Growth Mindset**

Teach boys with ADHD the power of a growth mindset, where challenges are seen as opportunities for growth and learning. In the classroom or at home, inspire them to embrace challenges, persevere through setbacks, and view mistakes as stepping stones towards success. By fostering a growth mindset, they develop resilience, self-belief, and a sense of accomplishment that boosts their self-esteem and fuels their personal growth.

A growth mindset is the ability to see challenges not as daunting obstacles but as exciting adventures waiting to be conquered. It is the belief that their abilities and intelligence can be developed through effort, practice, and the willingness to learn from mistakes.

Embracing a growth mindset empowers boys with ADHD to

view themselves as capable and resilient learners. They understand that their abilities can be developed and expanded over time with dedication and effort. They become more open to taking risks, exploring new ideas, and stepping out of their comfort zones. This mindset not only boosts their self-esteem but also instills a sense of accomplishment and fulfillment as they witness their own progress and personal growth.

- **Create a Safe Haven for Self-Expression:**

Provide boys with ADHD a safe and non-judgmental space where they can express themselves freely, like a cozy nook in the social landscape. Encourage them to share their thoughts, feelings, and experiences without fear of criticism or rejection. Validate their emotions and actively listen to their stories. By creating this sanctuary of self-expression, their self-esteem blossoms, and they feel seen and heard in a world that sometimes feels chaotic.

To start, lay the foundation by fostering open communication and active listening. Encourage them to share their thoughts and feelings through words, drawings, or any other medium that sparks their imagination. Let them know that their ideas are as valuable as treasures and that you are there as their trusty sidekick, ready to lend an ear and support them in their superhero quests.

When they open up, be there with your superhero cape of attentiveness. Listen to their tales, opinions, and concerns without interrupting or judging. Show them that their stories matter and that you're their biggest fan, rooting for their success. Give them high-fives of validation by acknowledging their experiences and showing empathy for their challenges. Let them know that they're not alone in this grand adventure, that you're right there beside them, ready to face any obstacle together.

Remember, building this fantastic safe haven takes time and patience, like constructing an elaborate fortress of trust and respect. It is a place where they feel free to be their authentic selves, like superheroes unmasked. But fear not, for as they experience the power of this sanctuary, their self-esteem will soar higher than a superhero flying through the sky. They will become stronger, more confident, and discover their true selves, ready to conquer any challenge that comes their way.

- **Cultivate Positive Self-Talk Seeds:**

Help boys with ADHD develop a garden of positive self-talk, where affirmations and encouraging words flourish. Teach them to replace negative thoughts with positive and empowering statements. Encourage them to recognize their efforts, celebrate their achievements, and embrace self-compassion. By nurturing positive self-talk, they can water the seeds of self-esteem and cultivate a strong and resilient self-image.

To start this, teach them the art of replacing negative thoughts with positive and empowering statements. It is like pulling out weeds and planting seeds of self-belief. Encourage them to be aware of their inner dialogue and catch any self-doubt or self-criticism that sneaks into their minds. Then, together, transform those negative thoughts into positive affirmations, like planting seeds of self-compassion and encouragement.

Nurture these positive self-talk seeds by showering them with attention and care. Teach them to recognize their efforts, no matter how small or large, and celebrate their achievements. It is like providing nourishing soil and abundant sunlight to help the seeds grow into beautiful, confident blossoms. Encourage them to acknowledge their progress and remind themselves of their unique strengths and capabilities.

As they tend to their garden of positive self-talk, they will witness the transformation of their self-image. Self-compassion and self-acceptance will become their nurturing sunlight, fostering a deep sense of self-worth and resilience. They will develop a more positive outlook on their abilities and potential, like delicate flowers reaching for the sky.

In this lush garden, they will learn to embrace self-compassion. Just like nurturing a delicate orchid, they will learn to treat themselves with kindness and understanding. Encourage them to be gentle with themselves, to forgive their mistakes, and to practice self-care. Remind them that they're deserving of love and acceptance, just as every beautiful flower in the garden is worthy of admiration.

In the end, building self-esteem and fostering positive relationships in boys with ADHD is like tending to an intricate plant. It requires patience, care, and lots of love. As we implement these strategies, let us nurture their self-esteem, cultivate their connections, and create a world where they flourish with confidence and thrive within

## Chapter 5

# Preparing Your Child for Success in School and Life

Continuing our adventurous journey through the social jungle, we now find ourselves at the entrance of a hidden path leading to this chapter. In this chapter, we will discover valuable insights and practical strategies to equip parents with the tools they need to guide their child with ADHD toward independence, resilience, and self-advocacy.

One important thing you will learn from this chapter will be the significance of fostering independence in our young explorers. Like teaching them to carve their own paths through the dense jungle, we will learn how to nurture their ability to take ownership of their actions and responsibilities. From practical tips on organization and time management to encouraging them to make informed decisions, we will uncover strategies that empower our children to thrive in their academic and personal pursuits.

Furthermore, we will embark on a quest to unlock the power of self-advocacy. Our children deserve to have their voices heard amidst the cacophony of the jungle. The author will guide us through empowering techniques to help them effectively communicate their needs, seek support when necessary, and advocate for themselves in both academic and social settings. By nurturing their self-advocacy skills, we provide them with the compass to confidently navigate the diverse landscapes of school and life.

So, fellow travelers, let us venture deeper into this chapter, prepared to uncover the treasures that lie within. With each step, we move closer to empowering our children with the skills they need to flourish in both school and the vast wilderness of life.

## 5 Tips for developing resilience and coping skills

What would a journey through this jungle of ADHD be without a couple trusty tips and tricks along the way? These tried-and-true tips will encourage growth in our boys with ADHD and make it so that they walk through life with ease. Let us get into it, shall we?

1. **Foster Problem-Solving Skills:**

For boys with ADHD, developing problem-solving skills is like handing them a treasure map to navigate the twists and turns of life. ADHD can sometimes make staying organized and focused feel like searching for buried treasure in a chaotic jungle. But fear not! By teaching them problem-solving skills, you are giving them the keys to unlock hidden solutions and emerge victorious.

As I have touched on in the previous chapter, encouraging your child to break down challenges into smaller, more manageable steps is like handing them a machete to clear a path through the dense foliage. They can take on one step at a time, conquering each hurdle and inching closer to their goal. It is like hacking away at the undergrowth, making way for clarity and progress.

Brainstorming possible solutions is like exploring a treasure trove of ideas. Encourage your child to let their imagination run wild, like a pirate searching for new adventures. Remind them that there is no such thing as a silly idea during brainstorming. It is a chance to think outside the treasure chest and consider all the possibilities that lie ahead.

Supporting your child in evaluating the outcomes of different solutions is like helping them decipher a map to find the hidden loot. Together, you can weigh the pros and cons, navigating the treacherous waters of decision-making. Will the outcome lead to golden rewards or a misstep into the quicksand? It is an exciting journey of exploration and critical thinking.

Creating structure and routines is like building a sturdy ship to sail through stormy seas. Establishing a consistent problem-solving routine provides stability and direction. It is like hoisting the sails and setting a course, ensuring that your child stays on track and avoids the whirlpools of distraction.

As Chapter 4 goes over in detail, visual aids and tools are like handy gadgets in their treasure-hunting toolkit. Charts, diagrams, and checklists become their trusty compass, guiding them through the maze of problem-solving. And just like a pirate with a map and a compass, they will be able to navigate their way to success.

2. **Encourage Self-Reflection:**

Fostering self-reflection is like giving our boys with ADHD a pair of superhero glasses that allow them to see beneath the surface of their own thoughts and actions. ADHD can sometimes make it challenging for them to tune into their own inner workings, but fear not! By encouraging self-reflection, you are empowering them to develop a deeper understanding of themselves and make more informed decisions.

Start by creating a relaxed and lighthearted atmosphere for self-reflection. Picture it as a secret hideout where they can retreat to contemplate the mysteries of their own minds. Encourage them to take a moment to pause, and reflect on their thoughts, feelings, and actions.

Help them identify their superpowers—those unique strengths and abilities that make them truly special. It is like unearthing hidden gems in the depths of a treasure cave. By recognizing their strengths, they gain a sense of confidence and can leverage those superpowers to tackle challenges with gusto.

But let us not forget about the areas for improvement, for even superheroes have room to grow! Guide them in identifying areas where they can enhance their skills or make adjustments. This is not about dwelling on mistakes or shortcomings, but rather about embracing the journey of personal growth. It is like upgrading their superhero gear, tweaking their gadgets, and fine-tuning their powers to become even more unstoppable.

Encourage them to explore their emotions like intrepid explorers charting uncharted territories. Help them recognize and label their feelings, understanding that emotions are like the wild creatures of the jungle—sometimes untamed but always providing valuable information. By acknowledging and understanding their emotions, they gain greater self-awareness and can make choices aligned with their values and well-being.

Self-reflection also involves learning from past experiences, just like a superhero studying their previous adventures to gather wisdom for future missions. Encourage your child to think about their actions and their consequences, fostering a sense of accountability and personal responsibility. This allows them to make more informed decisions and navigate the social jungle with greater awareness.

3. **Build Self-Regulation skills:**

As we have discussed several times within the pages of this book, regulating emotions with ADHD can be a daunting task. When emotions run high, encourage them to take a deep breath, and engage in calming techniques. It is like activating their superpowers of relaxation! Whether it is taking deep breaths, practicing mindfulness, or engaging in activities they enjoy, these tools help them find their calm amidst the storm.

Encourage them to express their feelings in healthy and constructive ways. Journaling can be their sidekick, to whom they pour out their thoughts and emotions. Talking with a trusted adult should also be advised if they are looking to find understanding and support. By providing outlets for expression, they gain a sense of release and clarity, like shaking off the weight of a heavy cape.

Teach them to identify their emotions as if they were decoding secret messages in the jungle. Help them understand that emotions are like colorful creatures roaming the wilderness of their minds, each with its own significance and purpose. By recognizing and labeling their emotions, they develop a greater understanding of themselves and others, allowing them to navigate the social landscape with more finesse.

Encourage them to embrace their emotions with a sense of playfulness and curiosity. Just like superheroes with incredible powers, their emotions are part of what makes them extraordinary. Remind them that every emotion serves a purpose and provides valuable information. It is like uncovering clues and solving riddles along their adventurous journey.

In the face of stressful situations, remind them to tap into their superpower of emotional regulation. Help them develop their own unique strategies for managing stress and anxiety. It could be listening to their favorite music, engaging in physical activity, or using visualization techniques. These tools become their trusty sidekicks, always ready to lend a helping hand when emotions become overwhelming.

And let us not forget the importance of humor! Laughter is their secret weapon, capable of diffusing tense situations and bringing a lightness to heavy hearts. Encourage them to find joy and humor in everyday moments, like a well-timed punchline or a playful dance.

## 4. Foster Social Support:

Fostering social support for boys with ADHD is like gathering up all the animals in the jungle, ready to join forces and conquer any challenge that comes their way. ADHD can sometimes make boys feel as though they are all alone, but with a little encouragement and guidance, they can build a network of friends, family, and support groups who have their back.

Teach your child just how helpful expressing their needs and asking for help can be. Help them understand that seeking support is a sign of strength, not weakness. It is like activating the powers of vulnerability and trust. Encourage them to share their problems, feelings, and wins with their support network, making it so that their team is always at their side!

On top of that, gently push your kid to take part in support groups or communities specifically catered to boys with ADHD. These groups can become their secret headquarters inside the jungle, a place where they can connect with others who share similar experiences and challenges. It is like finding a tribe of buddies who truly understand what they're going through. These groups provide a platform for sharing insights, strategies, and encouragement, fostering a sense of belonging and validation.

You should start by helping your child develop their communication skills, empowering them to express their needs and feelings effectively. Teach them the art of active listening and empathy, like a superhero using their superpower of understanding. Encourage them to be open-minded and receptive to the perspectives and experiences of others. By cultivating these skills, they not only strengthen their existing relationships but also forge new connections based on mutual respect and support.

Remember, fostering social support is an ongoing journey, much like an ever-expanding superhero universe. Encourage your child to nurture their relationships by spending quality time together, engaging in shared interests, and celebrating each other's successes. By fostering social connections and support, you create a safety net for your child, ensuring they never have to face challenges alone.

5. **Promote Healthy Lifestyle Habits:**

Promoting healthy lifestyle habits for boys with ADHD is like equipping them with a secret stash of jungle potions and elixirs that unlock their superpowers. Just as adventurers rely on these mystical concoctions to boost their strength and resilience, a healthy body and mind serve as the ultimate power-up for your child's journey.

Encourage your child to embark on daring physical expeditions, whether it is through sports, jungle hikes, or epic quests of fun fitness routines. These thrilling activities open up their hidden powers, releasing endorphins that boost mood, sharpen focus, and conquer anxiety like fearless explorers. Help them discover their favorite activities and make them a thrilling part of their routine, turning exercise into an exhilarating jungle expedition.

Sleep becomes their very own sanctuary - a realm where they replenish and recharge. Ensure your child sleeps between 8-10 hours each night, as it will improve their cognitive abilities, mood regulation, and overall well-being. Craft a bedtime routine that sets the stage for optimal sleep quality, a secret ritual that prepares them for a night of rest and rejuvenation.

Encourage your child to indulge in the bounty of nature's pantry, where they will discover an array of powerful fruits, vegetables, and other nutrient-rich treasures. Just as ancient tribes relied on nourishing diets to fuel their legendary feats, a well-balanced eating plan becomes the secret recipe for your child's mental clarity and physical prowess. Emphasize the importance of savoring whole grains, tropical fruits, vibrant veggies, lean proteins, and hearty healthy fats. Together, you'll embark on a culinary jungle adventure, unearthing nutritious and delectable treasures that turn mealtimes into epic feasts.

Guide your child through the dense foliage of nutritional knowledge, teaching them about the impact of different foods on their mental and physical powers. Enlighten them about the pitfalls of sugary or processed treats that can sabotage their focus and energy levels, like hidden traps lurking in the undergrowth. Empower them to make wise choices and listen to their body's secret signals, unlocking their superpower of self-awareness and wise dietary decisions

As they navigate the untamed wilderness of life, teach your child the art of managing stress. Help them use research backed techniques of deep breathing, mindfulness, and indulging in their favorite pastimes. Encourage them to seek refuge in creative outlets like crafting, playing music, or writing stories—mighty weapons that slay stress and release their emotional powers.

Remember, the journey of cultivating healthy habits is an ongoing quest. Lead by example, showcasing your own lifestyle and rallying the whole family to join in the quest for healthier practices. Along the way, celebrate even the smallest victories. By promoting these healthy habits, you'll unlock your child's true potential, allowing them to conquer the world around them with ease.

With a healthy body and mind as their trusty allies, your child will harness the strength and endurance needed to navigate the wilds, conquer adversity, and emerge as the hero of their own story. Together, you'll embark on a thrilling adventure, unleashing their full potential and paving the way for success in every corner of the jungle they explore.

## Fostering independence and self-advocacy

Ah, the grand quest of fostering independence and self-advocacy in boys with ADHD—a noble endeavor that holds the potential for great triumph and growth. Picture it as an epic adventure through the dense forests of life, where your child navigates the twists and turns with confidence and self-assuredness.

Why is it so important, you ask?

Well, as it turns out, when boys with ADHD embrace their independence, they become the masters of their own destiny. They learn to have faith in their abilities, make decisions, and take ownership of their actions. It is like bestowing upon them a magical talisman that unlocks their inner strength and resilience.

Encouraging independence means providing them with opportunities to spread their wings and take flight. Give them tasks and responsibilities that match their abilities, allowing them to explore their skills and discover their own unique strengths. Whether it is managing their daily routines, completing homework assignments, or tackling household chores, these endeavors become stepping stones on their heroic journey towards independence.

How can you foster independence and self-advocacy?

It is time to fasten your seatbelts and get ready for a wild ride as we dive into some quick tips and tricks that will have your child soaring to new heights of independence and self-advocacy in no time!

- **The Quest for Responsibility:** Assign age-appropriate tasks and responsibilities to your child. Start small and gradually increase the level of challenge. Whether it is feeding a pet, organizing their belongings, or helping with household chores, each accomplishment becomes a stepping stone towards independence.

- **The Adventure of Decision-Making:** Empower your child to make decisions on their own, within appropriate boundaries. Present them with choices and encourage them to weigh the pros and cons. For example, let them choose between two healthy snacks or decide which extracurricular activity they would like to pursue. This builds their decision-making muscles and nurtures their sense of autonomy.

- **The Magical Time Management:** Time management is a valuable skill for independence. Introduce your child to the wonders of visual schedules, timers, or alarms. Let them take the lead in planning their day, allocating time for tasks, play, and relaxation. By mastering the art of time management, they become the masters of their own destiny.

- **The Guild of Self-Awareness:** Teach your child about their unique strengths, challenges, and the impact of ADHD on their daily life. Help them develop self-awareness by encouraging reflection and open conversations. By understanding themselves better, they can advocate for their needs and communicate effectively with others.

- **The Fellowship of Self-Advocacy:** Role-play scenarios where your child needs to advocate for themselves. Create a safe space where they can practice expressing their needs, asking for help, or seeking accommodations. Equip them with scripts and phrases they can use confidently. Together, you can hone their self-advocacy skills and unlock their true potential.

- **The Potion of Communication:** Encourage open and

honest communication within your family. Create a supportive environment where your child feels comfortable expressing their thoughts, emotions, and concerns. Foster active listening skills by giving them your undivided attention when they speak. This strengthens their communication abilities and paves the way for self-advocacy.

- **The Quest for Reflection:** Encourage your child to reflect on their experiences and learn from them. Help them identify their strengths, areas for improvement, and strategies that work best for them. This cultivates a growth mindset, where they embrace challenges as opportunities for growth and resilience.

- **The Celebration of Achievements:** Celebrate your child's accomplishments, no matter how small. Acknowledge their efforts, progress, and growth along the way. Reward their independence and self-advocacy with praise, special treats, or engaging in activities they enjoy. By celebrating their triumphs, you reinforce their confidence and motivation.

Keep in mind, parents, fostering independence and self-advocacy is an ongoing expedition. Be patient, provide guidance, and celebrate each milestone reached. With these tips as your trusty companions, you and your child will embark on a thrilling adventure, embracing the power of independence and self-advocacy. Onward to greatness!

## Additional Resources

Preparing your boys with ADHD for success in school and life requires a toolbox filled with valuable resources and information. Fortunately, there are numerous sources of support available that can guide you on this epic quest. Think of yourself as the brave adventurer this time, embarking on a journey to equip your child with the tools they need to conquer challenges and soar to new heights.

- **Professional Organizations**

Professional organizations specializing in ADHD are like magical academies of knowledge, ready to guide you through the mystical realm of attention deficit/hyperactivity disorder. Think of them as the Hogwarts of ADHD, where you can find all the essential spells and potions to support your child's unique needs.

The Children and Adults with Attention-Deficit/Hyperactivity Disorder (CHADD) is like the Sorting Hat, sorting through the complexities of ADHD to provide you with a wealth of information. They offer webinars and conferences that feel like attending classes taught by the most brilliant wizards and witches. With their evidence-based strategies and up-to-date research, you will feel like you've discovered the secret library of ADHD wisdom.

The National Resource Center on ADHD is like the Room of Requirement, magically appearing whenever you need guidance. It is a treasure trove of resources that cater to parents, caregivers, and educators. They provide support networks that feel like joining a magical Order, where you can connect with fellow wizards and sorceresses who understand the challenges you face.

Together, these professional organizations form a powerful alliance, much like Dumbledore's Army, arming you with the knowledge and tools to face the challenges of ADHD head-on. They will teach you the spells to unlock your child's potential, the potions to address their specific needs, and the charms to create a supportive environment.

- **Parent Support Groups**

Parent support groups are pretty much the secret societies of understanding, where you can gather with fellow adventurers on the wild journey of parenting a child with ADHD. Think of them as a gathering of explorers, each with their unique abilities and experiences, ready to unite and conquer the challenges that lie ahead.

In these groups, you will discover a safe haven, a fortress of comfort, where you can ask questions without fear of judgment and seek advice from those who have wielded the sword of parenthood in the face of ADHD. It is a place where you can swap your parenting capes and don the armor of empathy, knowing that everyone within the group truly understands the triumphs and challenges you encounter.

These support groups are also pretty helpful with training for the future. You can learn from the collective wisdom of those who have ventured into the world of boys and ADHD before you. They offer a treasure trove of strategies, battle-tested techniques, and a little bit of magic to help you navigate the twists and turns of raising a child with ADHD.

- **Books and Publications**

Ah, books, the treasure chests of knowledge and imagination! When it comes to ADHD, there are numerous books and publications that can guide you through the enchanted forest of understanding. Think of them as magical tomes filled with wisdom, insights, and practical spells to help you navigate the twists and turns of raising a child with ADHD.

"Taking Charge of ADHD" by Russell A. Barkley is like a potion brewed by a master alchemist. It unveils the secrets of managing ADHD, offering practical strategies that are as effective as a wizard's wand. Barkley's words will empower you with a deeper understanding of ADHD, equipping you with the tools to guide your child on their epic quest for success.

"The ADHD Effect on Marriage" by Melissa Orlov is like a magical mirror that reflects the unique challenges faced by couples in the realm of ADHD. It delves into the intricate dance of relationships, helping you navigate the complexities and uncover the hidden strengths that lie within. With Orlov's guidance, you'll discover how to strengthen your bond and create a harmonious partnership, even in the face of ADHD's magical mischief.

These books, along with many others written by renowned experts, offer a blend of professional expertise and personal anecdotes. They provide a whole bunch of insights, strategies, and parenting techniques, akin to the teachings of ancient sages. As you turn each page, you'll uncover gems of knowledge and discover new paths to support your child's journey.

- **Educational Resources**

When it comes to supporting your child with ADHD in their academic endeavors, the school becomes a magical kingdom filled with resources and allies who are ready to join forces with you.

Collaborating with your child's school is probably the best thing you can do. Together, you'll uncover the power of tailored educational resources that will unlock your child's full potential! The teachers, counselors, and special education professionals are your wise guides, equipped with a deep understanding of ADHD and the strategies to help your child thrive.

They will talk about classroom accommodations that could create a supportive learning environment for your child. From preferential seating to extra time on assignments, these accommodations are like a customized spell book, designed to meet your child's specific needs and enhance their learning experience.

Individualized Education Programs (IEPs) are like magical maps that chart a unique path for your child's academic journey. With the help of the school's experts, you'll create a personalized plan that addresses your child's strengths and challenges. The IEP will guide your child through enchanted forests of learning, ensuring they receive the necessary support and adaptations to succeed.

School psychologists and behavioral therapists possess the wisdom of ancient sorcerers when it comes to managing behaviors and improving executive functioning skills. They will equip you with the necessary knowledge to help your child develop strategies for organization, time management, and self-regulation. These tools will empower your child to navigate the twists and turns of the academic realm with confidence and resilience.

- **Online tools and apps**

The world of online tools and apps is where technology becomes a trusty sidekick in your child's quest to conquer ADHD-related challenges. These digital wonders are designed to empower your child with organization, time management, and self-regulation skills.

Imagine wielding a task management app like Trello, where your child becomes the master of their own quest board. With its interactive and visually captivating interface, Trello transforms mundane tasks into exciting missions. Your child can create colorful cards, assign due dates, and move them across different boards, tracking their progress with a sense of accomplishment. It is like having a digital companion that keeps them on track and motivated throughout their adventures.

Habitica is another remarkable tool that infuses the spirit of gamification into the realm of productivity. By transforming everyday tasks into quests and rewards, Habitica turns your child's routine into an epic adventure. They can create their own character, level up by completing tasks, and earn virtual rewards for their real-life achievements. It is like having a loyal companion who accompanies your child on their journey, cheering them on and celebrating their victories.

And let us not forget Forest, an app that helps your child harness the power of focus and concentration. By planting virtual trees and setting a timer, Forest creates a serene environment where distractions are kept at bay. As your child stays focused on their tasks, their virtual forest flourishes, and they can witness the tangible results of their productivity. It is like having a magical forest guardian that safeguards their attention and helps them thrive.

These online tools and apps are like a magical inventory, brimming with options that cater to your child's specific needs and preferences. As you explore this realm, encourage your child to embrace the ones that resonate with them, ensuring that the technology becomes a helpful companion rather than a distraction.

- **Therapy and Counseling Services**

Enter the realm of therapy and counseling services, where the power of transformation and self-discovery awaits your child.

Professionals in these fields offer invaluable support to help your child navigate the challenges of ADHD and boyhood.

In the world of therapy and counseling, you are not alone. Skilled professionals provide the guidance and tools necessary to empower your child and your family. They become allies, offering a safe space where vulnerabilities are embraced, strengths are celebrated, and growth is nurtured.

One potent tool is cognitive-behavioral therapy (CBT), an approach that empowers your child with coping strategies and emotional mastery. Through the guidance of a skilled therapist, your child can embark on a quest to unravel the intricate workings of their thoughts, emotions, and behaviors. CBT provides them with a map to navigate through the labyrinth of ADHD-related challenges, teaching them how to reframe negative thoughts, manage impulsivity, and cultivate resilience. It is like discovering a hidden treasure chest filled with tools to conquer self-doubt, anxiety, and low self-esteem.

But the journey doesn't stop there. Family therapy shines as a beacon of support, inviting you and your loved ones to embark on a collective quest of understanding and growth. With the guidance of a compassionate therapist, family therapy becomes a sacred space where bonds are strengthened, communication is revitalized, and the unique dynamics of living with ADHD are navigated. Together, you embark on a quest to uncover strategies that foster harmony, empathy, and shared understanding. It is like joining forces with fellow adventurers, forging unbreakable bonds as you conquer the challenges that lie ahead.

Parents, it is important to remember that every child is unique, and what works for one may not work for another. Customize your strategies and approaches to fit your child's strengths and needs. By leveraging these resources and tapping into the knowledge and support available, you will become a seasoned hero, equipped with the tools necessary to guide your child towards a future filled with growth and success. Embrace the adventure and let the journey unfold!

# Conclusion

In the pages of this book, we have embarked on an extraordinary adventure, exploring the realm of ADHD and uncovering the tools and strategies that can empower your child with success and resilience. From understanding the unique challenges of ADHD to fostering self-reflection, promoting healthy lifestyle habits, and accessing valuable resources, we have traversed a path filled with insights, guidance, and a touch of levity.

Through the pages, we have discovered that ADHD is not a limitation but a superpower, and with the right support and understanding, your child can soar to new heights. We have learned that fostering independence and self-advocacy ignites their inner hero, enabling them to take charge of their own journey and confidently navigate the world around them.

We have embraced the power of community, connecting with

## Conclusion

fellow parents and joining forces with professional organizations and support groups. Together, we have found solace, shared experiences, and gleaned wisdom from those who have walked the same path. We have delved into the pages of books, uncovering practical strategies, parenting techniques, and deeper insights into ADHD's intricate workings.

We have talked about educators, counselors, and special education professionals, creating a powerful alliance to unlock your child's potential within the classroom and beyond. By harnessing the magic of technology, we have discovered online tools and apps that transform ADHD-related challenges into opportunities for growth, productivity, and self-regulation.

In the realm of therapy and counseling, we have witnessed the importance of cognitive-behavioral therapy (CBT) and family therapy. These allies have equipped your child with coping strategies, emotional resilience, and strengthened the bonds that hold your family together.

And as we reach the final pages of this book, let us remember that the journey doesn't end here. Your child's story continues to unfold, with each chapter bringing new challenges, triumphs, and growth. Embrace the power of self-reflection, encourage healthy lifestyle habits, and foster independence and self-advocacy. Seek out support from the resources available, both within your community and online.

Above all, remember that you are not alone on this quest. You are part of a vast community of parents, caregivers, educators, and professionals who are dedicated to supporting and empowering children with ADHD. Embrace the adventure, celebrate the victories, and learn from the setbacks. Together, we can navigate the twists and turns of ADHD, transforming the journey into a tapestry of strength, resilience, and extraordinary achievements.

I hope that this book will serve as a guiding light, illuminating your path as you prepare your child with ADHD for success in school and life. Embrace the adventure, and let your child's unique gifts and talents shine brightly. Their story is yet to be written, and with your unwavering support, they will author a tale that inspires, uplifts, and leaves a lasting impact on the world.

# Thank You

Before you leave, I'd just like to say, thank you so much for purchasing my book.

I spent many days and nights working on this book so I could finally put this in your hands.

So, before you leave, I'd like to ask you a small favor.

Would you please consider posting a review on the platform? Your reviews are one of the best ways to support indie authors like me, and every review counts.

Your feedback will allow me to continue writing books just like this one, so let me know if you enjoyed it and why. I read every review and I would love to hear from you.